Charikleia and I dedicate this book to e[...]
but like the cousins in the story, we liv[...]

Copyright © 2020 Elisavet Arkolaki, Charikleia Arkolaki

Translated into French by Nicolas Naillon

For permission requests and supplementary teaching material, please write to the publisher
at liza@maltamum.com www.maltamum.com

ISBN 9798710442968

My cousin and I look alike. My aunt and uncle say we look like siblings. My mommy and daddy say we look like siblings. My grandma and grandpa, the whole family, even our friends, say we look like siblings. More like twin sisters actually, like our mothers did when they were children.

Ma cousine et moi, on se ressemble beaucoup. Ma tante et mon oncle disent que nous nous ressemblons comme des sœurs. Maman et Papa aussi disent que nous nous ressemblons comme des sœurs. Ma grand-mère et mon grand-père, toute la famille, et même nos amis, disent que nous nous ressemblons comme des sœurs. De vraies sœurs jumelles même, comme nos mères lorsqu'elles étaient enfants.

When we were little, we lived next door to each other. To see her, all I had to do was cross the tall grass in front of our house, open the gate and enter her garden. We met every day and played all sorts of games.
She was my neighbor and best friend. But then she moved.

Quand nous étions petites, nous étions voisines. Pour la voir, je n'avais qu'à traverser l'étendue de haute pelouse devant la maison, ouvrir le portail et entrer dans son jardin.
On se rejoignait tous les jours pour jouer à toutes sortes de jeux. C'était ma voisine et ma meilleure amie.
Mais un jour, elle a déménagé.

Now she lives in a faraway land, and I miss her so much. Mommy said to try and find something positive no matter the circumstances. There's always something to be grateful for. And so I did. My cousin and I are very lucky. Despite the distance between us, we can still talk, play, and see each other often via video chat. We talk about everything!

Elle vit maintenant dans un pays très loin d'ici, et elle me manque énormément. Maman dit qu'il faut toujours voir le bon côté des choses, essayer de trouver du positif dans chaque situation et faire montre de gratitude. Alors c'est ce que j'ai fait. En fait, ma cousine et moi avons beaucoup de chance. Malgré la distance qui nous sépare, nous pouvons toujours parler, jouer et nous voir en appel vidéo. On parle de tout !

The last time we met online, she told me that it's winter and very cold there.
Everything is covered in snow. She snowboards, skis, and goes ice skating with her new friends.

La dernière fois que nous nous sommes retrouvées en ligne, elle m'a expliqué qu'en ce moment c'est l'hiver chez elle, et qu'il fait très froid. Tout est recouvert de neige. Elle fait du snowboard, du ski et du patin à glace avec ses nouveaux amis.

I told her that it's summer
and very hot here.

Moi, je lui ai dit qu'ici, c'est l'été
et qu'il fait très chaud.

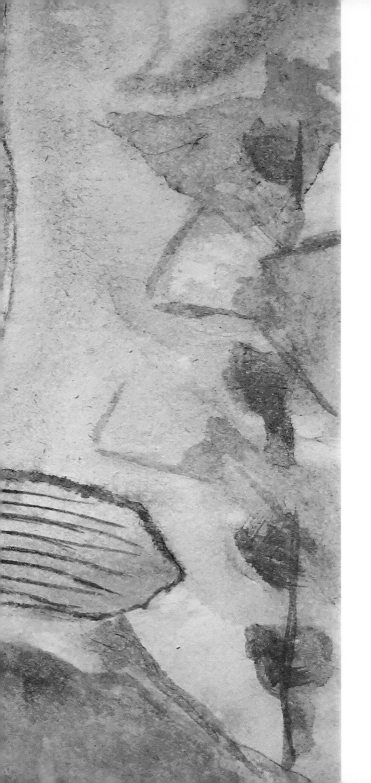

I swim and snorkel every day with our old friends, and we watch the most beautiful fish underwater.

Je nage et je fais du snorkeling tous les jours avec nos amis d'avant. Nous observons de magnifiques poissons sous l'eau.

Then, we spoke about animals. She said mammals with fur white as snow live in the northern part of her country: polar bears, arctic foxes, seals.

Ensuite, nous avons parlé d'animaux. Elle m'a dit que des mammifères au pelage blanc comme la neige vivaient dans le nord de son pays : des ours polaires, des renards arctiques, des phoques.

I had hoped she would also talk about monkeys, but it turns out they don't live there at all.

J'espérais qu'elle me parlerait aussi de singes, mais ils ne vivent pas du tout dans cette région apparemment.

She also asked about her pet which stayed behind with me. I answered that her cat is in very good hands and gets lots of cuddles and kisses.

Puis elle m'a demandé des nouvelles de son animal de compagnie resté ici avec moi. Je lui ai répondu que son chat était en de très bonnes mains et que je lui faisais plein de câlins et de bisous.

And I still go to the park on Sundays,
and feed the ducks we both love
so much.

Et je vais toujours au parc chaque
dimanche, pour nourrir les canards
que nous aimons tant toutes les deux.

Then, my cousin used some foreign words, and in an accent, I didn't recognize. I felt confused. She said she couldn't remember how to say "mountain", "rocks", and "river", and that she now talks more in her father's language.

Puis, avec un étrange accent, ma cousine a commencé à utiliser des mots étrangers que je ne connaissais pas. Je me suis sentie un peu perdue. Elle m'a dit qu'elle ne se souvenait plus comment dire "montagne", "pierres", et "rivière", et qu'elle parlait désormais davantage la langue de son père.

She explained that sometimes it's hard for her to find the right words in our language. I told her I understand. I'm also learning another language at school, and it should be fun to compare words from our different languages.

Elle m'a expliqué qu'il devenait parfois difficile pour elle de trouver les bons mots dans notre langue. Je lui ai répondu que je comprenais. J'apprends aussi une autre langue à l'école, ça pourrait être amusant de comparer les mots de nos différentes langues.

That is how we came up with the "Word Swap" painting game. My cousin painted a cactus, and then both of us said the word out loud. "Cactus" sounds the same in all our languages!

C'est comme ça que nous avons inventé le jeu "Échange de mots en peinture". Ma cousine a peint un cactus, et nous avons toutes les deux prononcé le mot à voix haute. "Cactus" se dit de la même façon dans toutes nos langues !

Her parents overheard us and joined the conversation. My aunt is a linguist and she told us that there are currently over 7,000 known spoken languages around the world! My uncle is a language teacher and he challenged us to swap a couple more words. We kept on going for a while with words like "flower", "water", "love", and "friendship".

Ses parents nous ont entendues et se sont joints à la conversation. Ma tante est linguiste et elle nous a appris qu'il existait plus de 7000 langues connues et parlées dans le monde ! Mon oncle, lui, est professeur de langues et il nous a donné quelques mots de plus à échanger. Nous avons continué un bon moment, avec des mots tels que "fleur", "eau", "amour" et "amitié".

Next time we video chat, I will share this painting I made for her. I would like to swap the word "home".

Lors de notre prochain appel vidéo, je lui montrerai cette peinture que j'ai faite pour elle. J'aimerais que nous échangions le mot "maison".

The Word Swap Game - Meet the children!

Erik, Nelly, Iason, Iria, Sadiq, Tariq, Vincent, Rukeiya, Lea, Hector, Victor, Orestis, Odysseas, Noah, Polyxeni, Lefteris, Alexis, Nikolas,Iahn, Chloe, Ioli, Rea, Nicolas, Sveva, Giuseppe, Zafiris, Dimitris, Periklis, Vaggelis, Andrea, Zaira, Philippos, Nefeli, Baby, George, Emmanuela, Mason, Ethan, Elijah, Oliver, Athina, Apolonas, Alexandros, John, Martina, Steffy, Thanos, Nikolai, Areti, Nikolai, Nina, Nicol, Joni, Mia, Emma, Stella, Artemis, Mirto, Antonis, Nicolas, Mihalis, Katerina, Nikos, Alexis, Liam, Olivia, Noah, William, Ava, Jacob, Isabella, Patricia, Hannah, Matthew, Ashley, Samantha, Maureen, Leanne, Kimberly, David, Marie, Vasilis, Yiannis, Kyra, Joakim, Alexander, Nikolas, Ellie, Sebastian, Sophie, Sabina, Stepan, Vasilis, Yiannis, Kyra, Youjin, Sejin, Okito, Magdalini, Nicoletta, Efimia, Di, Bia, Timo, Vittoria.

Unicorn - Ioli
Μονόκερος - Ιόλη

Ioli - Unicorn
Ιόλη - Μονόκερος

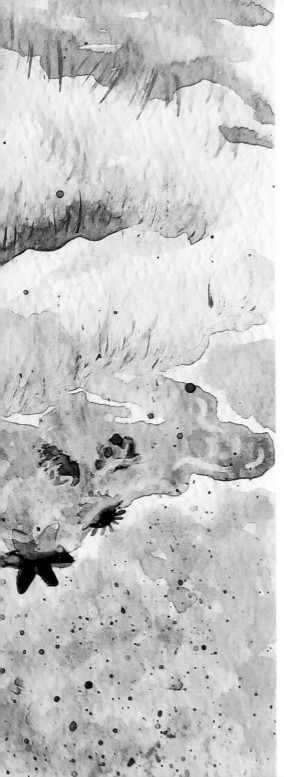

Dear Child,

I hope you enjoyed this story. If you'd also like to play the "Word Swap" game, ask an adult to help you, if needed, to write down your favorite word, and then draw or paint it. Your guardian can send me your painting via email at liza@maltamum.com, and I'll share it with other parents and children in my Facebook group "Elisavet Arkolaki's Behind The Book Club".

Dear Grown-up,

If you feel this book adds value to children's lives, please leave an honest review on Amazon or Goodreads. A shout-out on social media and a tag #CousinsForeverWordSwap would also be nothing short of amazing. Your review will help others discover the book, and encourage me to keep on writing. Visit eepurl.com/dvnij9 for free activities, printables and more.

Forever grateful, thank you!

All my best,
Elisavet Arkolaki

Printed in Poland
by Amazon Fulfillment
Poland Sp. z o.o., Wrocław

81878940R00021